THE WEATHER IS A GOOD STORYTELLER

Is maith an scéalaí an aimsir

The Weather is a Good Storyteller

Is maith an scéalaí an aimsir

A COLLECTION OF PROVERBS AND PHOTOGRAPHS

CARMEL FITZGERALD

and **BEN ELVES**

ashfield
PRESS

First published in 2004 by

ASHFIELD PRESS • DUBLIN • IRELAND

© Text Carmel Fitzgerald, 2004
© Photographs Ben Elves

ISBN: 1901658 37 6

Urraithe ag Foras na Gaeilge

Typeset in Diotima
Designed by
SUSAN WAINE

Printed in Ireland by
BETAPRINT LIMITED, DUBLIN

Introduction

PROVERBS OR SEANFHOCAIL are an integral part of world languages. They form the collected wisdom of generations and are handed down in both the oral and written traditions. The word seanfhocal literally means old word. The definition of proverb is a short, familiar saying expressing a supposed truth or moral lesson. Earl Russell, the 19th century British Whig Prime Minister, defined a proverb as the *"wit of one man and the wisdom of many."*

Proverbs in different languages show that the same kernel of wisdom transcends language and cultural differences. Often the same proverb may be found in many variants, due to the wide use of Latin as a means of communication throughout Europe in the Middle Ages. Folk proverbs are usually illustrated with homely imagery, household objects, farm animals, pets, the weather and the events of ordinary daily lives. The appearance in literary form is often adapted from the oral saying.

There are ancient Egyptian collections of proverbs dating from as early as 2500 BC. In Ireland, most of the earlier collections date from the mid 19th century. Robert Mac Adam, the Belfast antiquarian and Irish language activist, refers to *Tecosca Cormaic* or *Teagasc Cormaic*, ascribed to Cormac Mac Airt, one of the High Kings of Ireland. *The Teagasc* or Teaching of Cormac is a document of moral and practical instruction to his son, similar to King Solomon's address to his son in various chapters of the Book of Proverbs.

In *The Weather is a Good Storyteller* each proverb has a literal translation with a modern interpretation. The collection is representative of the four provinces of Ireland.

CARMEL FITZGERALD
Glenageary, Co. Dublin. October 2004

THE FIRST THING that struck me when I read these old Irish proverbs was how the majority of them concerned the weather and the land – mainly because people's livelihoods depended on them. Even today, the weather is talked about continually, and in a dramatic landscape like that of Ireland, the weather proves to be equally dramatic.

In those countries with a flat landscape, the sky can seem so far away. Here in Ireland, the landscape fits the clouds and the sky so perfectly that at times it can be hard to see where one begins and the other ends.

I have tried to show this in many of the photographs in this book, while in others, I have had to think of the timelessness of both the proverbs and the country in which they originate.

BEN ELVES

Clar, Redcastle, County Donegal

Ní hé lá na gaoithe lá na scolb.

A windy day is not for thatching.

There's a right time for everything.

Aithníonn ciaróg ciaróg eile.

One beetle recognises another.

Birds of a feather flock together.

Muna gcuirir san Earrach ní bhainfir sa bhFómhar.

If you don't sow in spring you won't reap in autumn.

If you don't learn when you're young you won't succeed later in life.

Leasú seacht mbliain brúcht mhaith sneachta.

A good fall of snow is fertiliser for seven years.

Heavy snowfalls are good for the soil.

Ní bhíonn a fhios ag duine cá luíonn an bhróg ar an duine eile.

No one knows where the boot pinches on another person.

No one knows another person's troubles.

Nuair a chruann an tslat is deacair í a lúbadh.

When the twig grows it is hard to bend it.

It's hard for an old person to change his ways.

19

Níl aon sean stoca nach bhfaigheann sean bhróg.

There is no old stocking that doesn't find an old boot.

There is someone for everyone.

Cad a bheadh súil agat a fháil ó bhó ach preab.

What would you expect from a cow but a kick.

Everything acts according to its nature.

Is maith an cúnamh an lá breá.

A fine day is a great help to everyone.

A sunny day lifts the spirit.

Is maith an mustard an sliabh.

The mountain is a good mustard.

A mountain walk whets the appetite.

Bail ó Dhia ar an obair.

God bless the work.

A traditional greeting to someone engaged in work.

Ritheann uiscí doimhne ciúin.

Deep waters run quietly.

Still waters run deep.

Giorraíonn beirt bóthar

Two shorten the road.

Company makes a journey pass more quickly.

Chomh gnóthach le cearc a mbeadh ubh aici.

As busy as a hen with an egg to lay.

Used to describe someone who can't relax.

D'imigh an t-im tríd an chálcheanann air.

The butter went through the colcannon on him.

His plans misfired.

Mar a leagtar an crann is ann a bhíonn na slisneacha.

Where the tree is felled that's where the chippings are.

Don't overlook the obvious.

Níor chuir Dia sceach i mbéal an chuain riamh.

God never put a bush in the mouth of the harbour.

God never stopped the wheels of progress.

Neantóg a dhóigh mé agus cupóg a leigheas mé.

A nettle stung me and a dock leaf cured me.

An old Irish cure.

A Dhia beannaigh don chéim a bhfuil mé ag dul, is beannaigh don chré atá féim chois.

God bless the step that I am taking and bless the soft earth beneath my feet.

An old Irish prayer.

Scuabann scuab úr go glan,ach tá fios ag an sean scuab ar na coirnéil.

A new broom sweeps clean but an old one knows the corners.

You can't beat experience.

Is maith an scéalaí an aimsir.

The weather is a good storyteller.

Time will tell.

Is leithne go mór cac bó má sheasann tú ann.

A cowpat is wide enough if you stand in it.

Perception and reality are two different things.

Nuair atá sneachta ar Néifinn tá sé fuar in Éirinn.

When there is snow on Nephin it's cold in Ireland.

Nephin Mountain in Co. Mayo is a good indicator of Irish weather.

Ní breac é go mbíonn sé ar an bport.

It isn't a trout until it's on the bank.

Don't count your chickens before they're hatched.

Níl aon tinteán mar do thinteán féin.

There is no hearth like your own.

There is no place like home.

Is ins an adhmad is boige a bhíonn an crann is cruaidhe.

It's in the softest wood you find the hardest knot.

A soft exterior can mask a hard interior.

Ni dhéanfadh an saol capall rása d'asal

The world could not make a
racehorse from a donkey.

You can't make a silk purse from a sow's ear.

Geimhreadh ceoch, Earrach reoch,
Samhradh grianmhar is Fómhar breá
biamhar.

A misty winter, a freezing spring,
a sunny summer and a bountiful
autumn.

An old Irish weather forecast.

Is faide do chuid féasóige ná do chuid intleachta mar a dúirt an sionnach leis an ngabhar.

More beard than brains as the fox said of the goat.

A strong physique is no guarantee of a keen intellect.

Bailíonn brobh beart.

Wisps gather a bundle.

Take care of the pennies and the pounds will look after themselves.

I ndiaidh a chéile is ea tógtar na caisleáin.

Castles are built one by one.

You must be patient when doing an important job.

Maireann an crann ach ní mhaireann an lámh a chuir é.

The tree remains but not the hand that planted it.

A tree will outlive generations of people.

71

Is glas iad na cnoic i bhfad uainn.

Faraway hills are green.

Distance lends enchantment.

Dá fhaid é an lá tiocfaidh an tráthnóna.

No matter how long the day the evening will come.

Nothing lasts forever.

75

Má tá céad gnó againn tá céad ló againn.

If we have a hundred things to do we have a hundred days to do them.

There is no point in trying to do things in a rush.

*An ghrian ag scoilteadh na gcrann agus an
préachán ag cur a theangan amach.*

The sun splitting the trees and the
crow with his tongue out.

A traditional description of a hot, sunny day.

Má dhíolann tú an capall, ní dhíolann tú an srian ná an diallait.

When you sell a horse you don't sell the saddle or the bridle.

Pisreog (*superstition*)

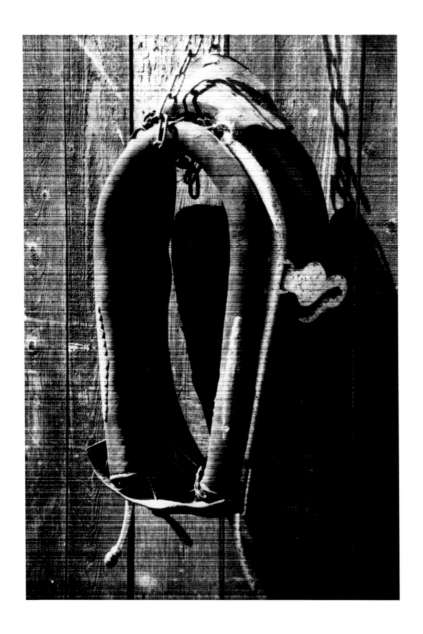

Caitheann síor-shileadh an chloch.

Continuous weathering wears the rock.

By persevering at something we succeed.

Tá eirbeall an chait sa ghríosach.

The cat's tail is in the hot ashes.

Sign of approaching bad weather.

Is é an sruthán éadoimhin a labhrann go dána.

It's the shallow stream that speaks boldly.

Empty vessels make most noise.

Ná déan dánaíocht ar an bhfarraige.

Don't make bold with the sea.

Respect the sea.

Is minic a bhíonn an t-úll dearg go holc ina chroí.

Many a red apple is rotten to the core.

Appearances can be deceptive.

Éist le tuile na habhann agus gheobhaidh tú breac.

Listen to the flow of the river and you will catch a trout.

Patience pays dividends.

An turas is faide sa saol tosnaíonn sé le coiscéim bheag amháin.

The longest journey in life starts with one small step.

Is maith é an bád a dhéanann amach an caladh a d'fhág sé.

It's a good boat that finds the harbour it left.

It's good to remember our origins.

Nior bhris focal maith fiacail riamh.

A good word never broke a tooth.

No bad can come of a kind word.

Fál maith a dhéanas comharsana maithe.

A good hedge makes for good neighbours.

Clear boundaries make for good relations.

Lá millte na móna lá fómhar an chabáiste.

The rain that destroys the turf can cause cabbage to grow.

What's bad for one thing can be good for another.

103

Is caol mar a ritheann sruth an ádha ach is ina thuillte móra a thagann an mí-ádh.

The stream of good fortune flows narrowly but misfortune comes in floods.

Troubles never come singly.

Go n-éirí an bóthar leat.

May the road rise with you.

Have a good journey.

PHOTOGRAPH LOCATIONS

SOURCES

Seanfhocal do gach ócáid. A seanfhocal for every occasion. Séan Ó hÓbáin. Ó hÓbáin 1988.

Seanfhocail na Mumhan. An Seabhach. 1926 an céad eagrán. An Gúm 1984, 2003.

The Poolbeg Book of Irish Proverbs. Fionnuala Williams. Poolbeg Press 1992.

Seanfhocail as Acaill. Tony Catherine Antoine William. *Cló Iar-Chonnacht.* Indreabhán 1995.

Sean-fhocla Chonnacht. Tomás S. Ó Máille. Oifig an tSoláthair. Baile Átha Cliath; 1948-1952.

ACKNOWLEDGEMENTS

Ba mhaith liom buíochas a ghabháil leis na daoine seo leanas
Bríd De Búrca B.A., Doctor Barry McCrea, Doctor Caitríona Ó Torna